Grace Notes
Loving Thoughts from
GRACE LIVINGSTON HILL

Barbour Books, Westwood, New Jersey

© 1991 by Barbour and Company, Inc.

Published by Barbour and Company, Inc., P.O. Box 1219, Westwood, New Jersey 07675.

Typesetting by Typetronix, Inc., Cape Coral, Florida

ISBN 1-55748-251-9

Printed in the United States of America

1   2   3   4   5 /   96   95   94   93   92   91

If instead of a gem, or even a flower, we could cast the gift of a lovely thought into the heart of a friend, that would be giving as the angels give.

George MacDonald

The Lord knows the end from the beginning, and nothing is surer than that He uses His children to carry out His plans.

"No word He hath spoken
Was ever yet broken."

Conscience, working all alone, is a very uncomfortable and disagreeable companion, and often accomplishes for the time being nothing beyond making his victim disagreeable.

You take a diamond and throw it down in the dirt and filth, and put your foot on it and grind it in, and leave it there, sinking and soiling, day after day, year after year, and when somebody comes along and picks it out, how much will it gleam for Him at first? Yet the diamond is there.

"Peace with God!" It expresses so much! Peace is greater than joy, or comfort, or rest.

Mine is the doing when He says the word, but His is the bringing to pass.

A sweet-faced cooing baby is an exquisite bit of enjoyment for anybody.

What a fearful world it would be if things just happened, with nobody to manage or control!

"Diligent in business, serving the Lord." There is no period dividing these. I long ago discovered that I could make a bed and sweep a room for His sake, as surely as I could speak a word for Him.

I know people who suppose it would be almost irreverent to take their domestic bewilderments to Christ. *I* cannot think what kind of a friend they imagine Him to be, if they are afraid to go to Him with everything.

Although the Lord is gracious and forbearing, and kindly gives me the work to do here and there for Him, He can, when He chooses, get along entirely without any help.

You may often speak words which spring up, and bear fruit that reaches up to *God*; though you do not know it, and will not, until in heaven you take your crown, and question why there are so many stars.

The heart must understand that whatever the Lord directs it intends to do, or there is no opening of the door for Him.

To God, nothing that an immortal soul can say, appears trivial.

There is no place on the road so dark but that the Bible can light you through.

God never promised to compromise with his own, never promised to hear a prayer which began with an "*If.*" Entire consecration means all the "ifs" thrown down at the feet of the Lord are for Him to control as He will.

*I*s it so strange a thing that the *L*ord can keep *H*is own!

It is wonderful, after all, how rarely in this wicked world we meet with other than respect in answer to a frank avowal of our determination to be on the Lord's side.

Individual effort is so necessary that I have thought perhaps the Holy Spirit turns our thoughts most directly toward one person at a time, so that we may concentrate our efforts.

$\mathcal{I}$ don't know how a thoughtful man can ever reject the idea of an overruling Providence.

Never mind whether you are now one of His children or not; claim the place of a child because you need to be, and wish to be, and mean to be one from this moment.

There has many a thing been accomplished in this world that never would have been, had people settled it in their minds that it couldn't be done before they had made vigorous efforts to do it.

*I*sn't it pleasant to think that in all those little things *H*e is watching over you, and that you make *H*im glad when you do them well?

What a salvation! *Able* to forgive transgression, to cover sin, to remember it no more.

You can find plenty of work if you look for it; only don't look too far, because it is the little bits of things, which come right in your way, that Jesus wants you to do.

You don't know what a relief it is to go right to the *Lord* with your worries.

I take it that *God* permits all faithful service to be for *His* glory.

Of course some change must come; nothing ever stayed for any length of time, just as it was; but what would the change be? It came in an unexpected manner, perhaps that is the common way with changes.

Every woman owns a little piece of the world; I do, so does everybody, why can't each one look out for her own little corner?

It is His own voice speaking. Go to Him for help, and as sure as the sun shines above these clouds you will get just what you need.

*S*uppose Christ should forgive only those who had treated Him well; would you be forgiven to-day?

Are you quite happy as a Christian?
Do you find your love growing stronger
and your hopes brighter from day to day?

"If our faith were but more simple,
    We should take Him at His word,
And our lives would be all sunshine
    In the sweetness of our Lord."

My dear friend, you have really no right to set a different time from one that your Master has set. Don't you know that His time is always now?

Sometimes the people whom we meet but once, with whom we really have very little to do, are given a word to say, or an act to perform, that shall influence all our future lives.

We are all too willing to be conquered, not willing to reach after and obtain the settled and ever-growing joys of the Christian.

Now what you need to remember, is, that the Lord is your father, whether you choose to own Him or not; and He has a right to your love, and your help.

Conversion is change of heart, and a heart given up to the reign of Christ, the supreme desire being to please Him, will, at the outset, be a very different heart from the one that was given up to the reign of self.

If my Christian life were so marked a force that all who came in contact with me felt its influence, it would be natural to speak of it, when my friends chanced to mention my name.

There's a thing to remember; that you don't belong to yourself at all; and are bound to do the best you can with your time, and strength, and everything.

There is nothing that He cannot forgive, and nothing that He cannot help you to do, if it is right that you should do it.

Did you ever tell Him all about it? Of course He knows, yet His direction is that for our sakes we tell Him the story.

"God will not call me to account for your undone work, only my own."

Is it possible that I have been one of those faithless disciples, rebuking, or at least ignoring, the presence of one of His little ones, while I reached out after fruit that I dared to think was of more importance!

*I*t doesn't seem to me that it is money, or time, or strength, or talent, that is lacking, it is the consecrated heart.

The man who seems to me the most worthy of contempt, is the one who has not sufficient moral courage to break a promise after he discovers that it ought never to have been made.

We depend too much on tact and too little on God's spirit. "Open thy mouth and I will fill it," is a promise that applies to more places than a prayer meeting, I think.

I know *I* love the Lord, and *I* know that *He* will not destroy me, for *I* have in my heart the assurance of *His* promise.

You will find that it needs precisely the same help to meet trifles that it does to conquer mountains of difficulty. The difference is in degree, not in kind.

I believe a consecrated life will be honored by the Lord in whatever channel He gives it talent to develop.

If people only would influence each other just as much as they could, and just as high as they could, what a wonderful thing this living would be!

Of course you cannot help these bitter feelings; do you suppose He expects you to do so? If you could make your heart right yourself, where would be the need of His help?

It is grand to think that even the street-car driver can drive for the glory of God.

"Do with thy might whatsoever thy hand findeth to do," is our commission, you know, and in order to find things, we have to look for them.

If I belong to Christ, I belong, don't I? There is no half-way service possible.

When I feel particularly tried with a person, I shall know that I am myself at fault, and shall ask God for a special view of my own heart concerning it.

A great deal of money and a great deal of force, which might do wonders elsewhere, are wasted on dress.

The fact is, that to sit in a pleasant room, among one's friends, and discuss the inconsistencies of Christians, is one thing; and to go out into the world in the thick of the fight, and live consistently, is quite another.

Since God has called us to honorable positions, even to be " co-laborers," shall we not rejoice in the honor?

A great sorrow is a wonderful educator.

$\mathcal{I}$t is, perhaps, to be questioned whether loneliness is, after all, demoralizing in its effects.

It is possible that you have not come in close contact with Christ's intimate friends. There are degrees in friendship, you know.

What we need most to overcome is the idea that there is anything wicked in talking about religion in an everyday tone, as we talk about other topics of absorbing interest.

If the Lord Jesus Christ can forgive him, I think we ought to be able to do so.

If we want to hear how living, growing Christians talk, we must frequent the places where we shall be likely to find them.

$\mathcal{I}$ wonder when the world will learn that promises are solemn things, and that living is serious business, and that when we are young we are not called upon to decide questions which belong to mature judgments.

When a sensible person has made a misstep, the thing for him is to undo as much of the mischief as he can; as quickly as he can; it is the only way he has of showing the difference between himself and a fool.

We must guard against a temptation to do evil, that good may come.

When I am conversing with any person what is my habitual theme?

What gorgeous coloring and delicate tracery in the leaves! Does it ever occur to you to wonder that such great skill should have been expended in just making them look pretty to please our eyes?

Justified! Not because I have done right; not because my judgment is correct; not because of any act of mine in any direction save that one trusting in my Lord, justified by faith!

It is a strange thing, but how can we help believing it to be actually the case, that people who would be shocked at the idea of violating their word to their fellow-men yet seem to ignore, without much trouble of conscience, the most solemn obligation made to God!

There is a sunlight so high and strong
that the clouds of this world cannot
reach it.

I try to remember that Christ knows all, and He loves me, and He is all-powerful; and yet He leads me through this dark road; therefore it must be right.

I believe that religion should have sufficient power over us to change all our tastes and plans in life, fitting them to the Saviour's use.

He sees the way plainly and He will lead us right through the thickets to the sunlight of His eternal presence.

I really believe that the Lord, when He said, "Give, and it shall be given unto you, good measure, pressed down and shaken together, and running over, shall men give into your bosom," meant just what He said.

It is God's world, and He made your little children. You may be sure He has a place for them, both in this world and in Heaven.

If God from His infinite height, can look down upon all the world, having the same wonderful, patient, persistent love for all mankind, what am I that I should not give my utmost strength for the poorest and meanest of His creatures?

We are all set apart, given to Him to use as He will. The trouble is that so many of us take back the gifts, and use our time and our tongues as though they were our own.

It would be a pity to get ready for only
one world when the other is so near by.

I wonder if people realize that they can arrange flowers in such a manner as to glorify the Lord of the garden.

The Lord sees the heart; and little seeds of loving kindness to one's neighbor, whether he be next door or across the ocean, may be in many hearts, unknown to us.

The heart of Christ is for each, as if each were alone in all the world the object of His care.

Do you think that Christians whose rule of life reads: "Whatsoever ye do, do all to the glory of God," have any right to go to social gatherings, or anywhere else, separated from this end?

Didn't you give Him your tongue when you gave Him yourself? And yet you are fortunate if you have not dishonored Him with it many a time.

It is easier to do things which you like,
and which in a sense are natural to you,
than it is to do what goes utterly against
the selfish side of your nature.

They aren't worth lifting a finger for. And yet, how can I help remembering that if the Lord Jesus had said that of us, and stayed up there in His glory, we should have been utterly without help or hope to-day?

An awakened conscience toyed with,
is a very fruitful source of misery.

I bless *Him* that *I* may constantly serve, whether *I* am wiping the dust from my table, or whether *I* am on my knees.

I doubt whether we should wait always for clear ways; perhaps we are expected to go creeping along in the dark. Satan has ways and doesn't scruple to use them.

I have met people who, it seemed to me, would rather trust their "rainy day fund" than the Lord.

*Y*our soul, remember, was worth the death of the Son of God. See that you make your life worthy such a sacrifice as that.

There is no trade on earth so easy to learn as grumbling.

I pity the man who has not brain power enough, and insight into the future enough, to be willing to be anchored in God.

Will He not be pleased with even my little bits of efforts if He knows that my sincere desire is to save souls for His glory?

We must feel some little measure of the same love for a soul, that the Lord Jesus does when He calls after it, else how can we hope to reach it?

"There is no desolation of heart to those who part at night to meet again in the morning."

When the church and the world start out to walk hand in hand, it is a curious thing that it is always the world that sees the inconsistencies, and laughs, and always the church that is blind.

More things than some people dream of, are going on in this world of ours.

The Sabbath is a blessed day of rest; and to think that the Lord gives a wonderful promise to them that keep it!

Do you think we ought to have an "anything but that," between the Lord and our prayers?

One reason why our friends are not converted is because we, their leaders, walk so crookedly that we keep them all the time stumbling over us.

Where would be the church of Christ
without its living, working members?

Don't allow yourself for one moment to limit the power and the grace of a Saviour. Remember He is "mighty to save."

I wonder how I should feel if I should go to heaven and meet one of those whom I ought to have known in the church on earth, and the Lord should see that we were strangers!

The fact is, we must learn to work for Christ, and not set up business for ourselves, and still expect Him to give the wages.

So many things in this world squeak for
the want of a thoughtful hand to admin-
ister a drop of oil.

I wonder when the Lord's own people will awaken to the fact that there are no trivial things in life? that there are no passing moments but what decide the eternal destinies of souls?

God is on your side, *He* will surely deliver you if you trust in *Him*; if you turn from *Him* how can *He* help you?

When you accepted Christ as your Friend, did you not engage to take some things on trust — to believe that what you could not see, was yet clear to the eye and the heart of your Saviour, and that He ruled?

There is just One who fought a battle
with Satan and came off victor, and
there never will be another.

In Him are safety and everlasting strength, and outside of Him is danger.

God bless the souls who, capable of rising to the heights which belong to immortality, yet think of kitchen fires and breakfasts.

We shall probably never know, on this side, how far the prayers of the mothers at home reach.

I think sometimes our Heavenly Father does just as we do with the children. He lets us stumble in a place where it is not too hard, so that we will learn what it is to obey.

The Lord knows you; knows just what place He has set you in; just how many people you can touch with your influence, and just what He is going to do with them all.

He has chosen us for His own, that we have been bought with a price, that we are held as infinitely precious in His sight, and that, therefore, we must set a high estimate on our own importance, and live accordingly.

Utter shipwreck of human happiness
is rarely, thank God, a necessity; even
though grievous blunders have been made.

Life is full of victories, and so long as we have a sure Captain to carry on the warfare, and know there will be victories, why should we be so disturbed about it?

If you belong to the *Lord Jesus,* surely *He* has work for you, and is able to point it out, and to fill your heart with satisfaction while you do *His* bidding.

We care for anything for which we work, and especially for which we sacrifice a little, you know.

I tremble for any man whose will is not anchored on the rock Christ Jesus.

Suppose we actually bore on our hearts the individual griefs of the world? How long would our poor bodies be in breaking under the strain?

Poor, tired heart. Don't you think that the Lord Jesus can rest you anywhere except by the way of the grave? Don't you hear His voice calling to you to come and rest in Him this minute?

There is so much religion in these days
that wants to be done up in pink cotton
and laid safely away from human sight
and sound.

It is easier to be good for others than it is for one's self.

It is a blessed thing that the just God is more tender and pitiful than men and women.

It is a strange thing, and a solemn thing to realize how unwittingly the seed of unbelief may be sown in a young heart.

When we stop and consider it, life, for the most part, is made up of little things. It is only the occasional which is startling in its magnitude.

I think if I could help to lead one person to understand and love the Lord Jesus Christ as much even as I, it would be ambition enough to fill a lifetime.

I wonder if everything about us, rightly
managed, would become a talent?

What wonderful rewards *God* may
have in store for even our smallest efforts
made for *His* sake!

I wonder to what extent the gracious
Spirit of God hovers near to suggest and
help those who never ask for His help?

I have been wondering how many of us are children of the same family traveling towards home, and failing to recognize the kinship on the way.

I never like to fight Satan with his
own weapons, he understands everything
pertaining to his business so much better
than we do.

I have unquestioning faith in the truth that even our mistakes *He* will overrule for our good.

"If you do not try to understand the people who are of another world than yours — to, in short, 'put yourselves in their places,' occasionally — how do you expect to be other than narrow and cold in your charities?"

A very little child can learn to love the Saviour.

It is better to give over planning the side that your arm is too weak to reach, and learn to trust.

Only think of it, whiter than snow! That is our privilege, to stand before God so white that even the whitest thing we know is shadowed, in comparison; and yet how little we try for it; how little of the whiteness we are willing to accept. We seem rather anxious to have the soiled garments left about us.

But do you think it is wise to spend your time in studying the imperfect copies, without looking at the perfect pattern?

Who will undertake to describe a soul?

You cannot see the heart. Only the Lord can see that, and it is only the Lord who has, therefore, a right to judge.

"But one must stand somewhere. Either you are willing to try to please the Lord Jesus Christ to-day, or else you are not willing. There is no middle ground."

It is surprising how many trials we do succeed in pushing through, and coming out alive on the other side!

A year is only a half-hour in Heaven.

I doubt if there are any chains harder
to break than sleepy ones.

God meant that the human will should be a great engine for good, but the human will perverted, is a rotten plank, on which one's weight cannot be trusted.

$\mathcal{I}$f you find there is the least doubt in
your mind as to the right or wrong of a
certain path, give Christ the benefit of the
doubt and you will surely be right.

If all honest unbelievers would but stop their reasoning, trying to plan out God's work for Him, and go to Him with the whole story, how quickly it would silence all doubt. For faith is the gift of God.

*S*ome sorrowful places there may be for your feet and mine on our journey home. Bear the thorns of the way in patience, for they are only on the way through the woods; not a thorn in the home.

Remember that no early mistake can be righted by adding to it a later and a graver one.

If you could be sure that the hand of the Lord was really in every phase of life, how greatly would it tone and temper all the experiences thereof!

I should like to know if even a little knowledge isn't better than ignorance! Suppose a stream isn't very deep; if it is water that we need, it is much better than no stream at all, isn't it?

The Lord met Saul and gave him wonderful salvation, but He didn't save him from many a future trial and pain. He never promised to do so.